# PARIS

## A PICTURE BOOK TO REMEMBER HER BY

Designed by
DAVID GIBBON

Produced by
TED SMART

CRESCENT

# INTRODUCTION

Many years before there was France, even before there was a race known as the French, there was Paris. On an island in the middle of the then turbulent waters of the River Seine, a group of Celtic tribesmen known as the Parisii settled to form a solid island home that survives today under the magical name of the 'Île de la Cité'. This island is the symbolic heart of Paris for it is from the Kilomètre Zéro, a brass compass-like star embedded in the pavement outside the Cathedral of Notre-Dame that all the city's distances are measured. More than any other part of Paris this island proclaims history and tradition; here the Roman legions of Julius Caesar established a permanent garrison half a century before the death of Christ and here for centuries the succeeding French kings installed themselves in the great stone palace, parts of which still stand near the western tip. The city's oldest buildings like Notre-Dame, the first of the French Gothic churches and one of the most beautiful, and the Louvre, once a royal palace and now one of the most richly endowed museums in the world, cluster on and around this island heart from which in the course of time the early foundations of the Paris of today spilled over onto both river banks to form a city, of which every stone seems steeped in history. The 17th century Porte Saint Denis for example, records the victories of Louis XIV, in the Place de la Concorde the Luxor obelisk brought from Egypt by Louis Philippe stands where once the dreaded guillotine awaited its victims and the mighty Pantheon is built on a site which was once that of a Roman temple to Diana and subsequently a medieval convent. The vestiges of a rich past are everywhere. Even just outside the city proper, Versailles, a quarter-mile long palace of pink and cream stone in the style of the classical period of French Renaissance with its lavish stucco, frescoes and tapestries presents a breath-taking vision of wealth, splendour and artistry.

Paris as a whole is a living work of art. From the pavement artists of Montmartre to the Leonardos of the Louvre, from the Left Bank 'bavardiers' to the masters of the Comédie Française, from the statues of the Tuileries to the masterpieces of the Musée du Jeu de Paume, Paris's cultural life is unbelievably rich and, since French culture finds its most complete expression in the visual and dramatic arts, it is not surprising that in this her principal city and its environs there are no less than 51 theatres and 107 museums.

Among Paris's great cultural centres, the Opéra, the largest theatre for opera in the world, is a spectacle in itself with its onyx-balustraded grand staircases, marble foyers, glittering chandeliers and, since 1966, a fresco by Chagall. Yet it is perhaps the Comédie Française which more than any other institution epitomizes the ideals of French civilization, for in providing a magnificent setting for the great classics of French theatre from Molière and Racine to Anouilh and Giraudoux, it gives expression to the classical ideals of patriotism and courage and to the quality of life and language so beloved by the French.

Because of its many artistic and architectural treasures Paris has been likened to a vast museum but the comparison is made void by the fact that the city is a living entity that continues to evolve in a way which provokes traditionalist criticism for its striking modernity but which, nevertheless, incorporates architecture of superb advanced design. The unclad metal truss tower of Gustave Eiffel, built for the Exhibition of 1889, in a sense began modern Paris. Composed of 12,000 metal parts fastened together by two and a half million rivets, it rises 984 feet above the Champs de Mars (and a futher eight inches in warm weather). Yet it weighs only 7,000 tons and with its four 'feet' covering an area of more than two acres, is calculated to exert no greater pressure than a man seated in a chair. More recent but equally striking are the high-rise futuristic buildings of the Quartier de la Défense, among them the Centre National des Industries et des Techniques with its spectacular swooping vault covering an area of 980,000 square feet, with only three points of support. Since the 1970s also, the slender 58 storey Tour Montparnasse presides over the Paris skyline but, like the city's older buildings these innovations have all been touched by the same love of elegance that has made Paris the fashion centre of the world and that has transformed even the subway stations into artistic masterpieces. All too, are harmonized by an all-pervasive atmosphere of verve and zest for living.

Despite the fact that Parisian beauties still perform the can-can at the Moulin Rouge and disrobe with admirable artistry in the Crazy Horse Saloon, Paris today by comparison with cities like Amsterdam or Stockholm is almost sedate. Yet few cities have such a sense of joie-de-vivre. With its innumerable shops, bars, cafés and restaurants, Paris is a living testament to the fact that the French enjoy good living and good food, for here is a gourmet's paradise. In the Rue Royale for example, the famous Maxim's provides unsurpassed cuisine in surroundings of an elegance that has not changed since the Belle Epoch while in contrast to it, but equally famous, La Coupôle in Montparnasse, a huge restaurant with something of the atmosphere of a railway station, will serve a superb but moderately-priced meal into the early hours of the morning. The opportunities for self-indulgence are endless. It is perhaps the street cafés which hold the greatest appeal however…cafés which line the great boulevards and squares and which seem to pop up on every possible street corner. It is here that the Parisians themselves spend so much of their time, dreaming, chatting and watching other people watch them and it is here also that much of the political, cultural and artistic life of France is said to have been engendered, for cafés like the Deux Magots have long been the meeting place of philosophers, writers and artists. It seems somehow appropriate that in a city which has been described as a 'celebration of the marriage of reason and romance' so much intellectual activity should be conducted in an essentially romantic atmosphere…and Paris is indisputably romantic. There are many who find the forthright logicality of the Parisians disconcerting but for those in quest of romance, this is more than compensated for by the vision of the gleaming white domes of the Sacré Coeur silhouetted against the night sky or of Notre-Dame set amongst the floodlit waters of the River Seine. It is settings such as these that have made Paris the very symbol of romance and the artistic inspiration of the world.

Sun sets *left* behind the imposing towers of the once notorious Palais de Justice, a complex of buildings which include the dreaded Conciergerie where Marie Antoinette awaited execution.
Most famous of all the landmarks of this magnificent city, the Eiffel Tower *overleaf* soars 984 feet above the Paris trees.

Commanding the Place Charles de Gaulle, from which twelve imposing avenues radiate to form a star, the majestic Arc de Triomphe *on these pages and overleaf* was first commissioned by Napoleon in 1806. After his fall it stood unfinished until Louis Philippe saw to the completion of this awe-inspiring monument, which at 50 metres is twice as high as the Arch of Constantine which inspired it.

On Armistice Day in 1920, the Unknown Soldier was buried beneath the centre of the arch *right* and each evening the flame of remembrance is rekindled by a different patriotic group.

Possibly most famous of the wide avenues which converge at the Arc de Triomphe, the Champs-Élysées *on these pages,* which under the Second Empire was the street of luxurious town houses, today parades a seemingly endless succession of cafés, nightclubs, elegant shops and cinemas, which have retained the atmosphere of luxury suggested by its name.
*Overleaf:* Beyond the powerful watersprays of the Palais de Chaillot rises the iron lattice of the Eiffel Tower.

Built for the International Exposition of 1889 in defiance of the opposition of many who believed it to be ugly or unsafe, or both, the Eiffel Tower was saved from demolition after the expiry of the exposition concession by demonstration of its value as an antenna for the newly developed radio and now forms an integral and much-loved part of the Paris landscape.

Paris has been a Christian city for 1500 years and its churches must rank among its greatest wonders. Of these Notre-Dame *on these pages and overleaf,* one of the oldest, is also one of the most beautiful. Begun in 1163 on the site of a Roman Temple on the Île de la Cité, it is constructed in the shape of a Latin cross with magnificent flying butresses and spires, so vast that their weight has caused this incredible building to sink more than three feet in the course of the ages.

Viewed from the spire of Notre-Dame the Paris skyline *above* is crowned by one of the most indelibly Parisian landmarks, the Sacré Coeur. Since 1919 the gleaming white domes of this exotic Basilica have presided over the picturesque buildings and colourful characters of Montmartre and its Place du Tertre *these pages and overleaf.*

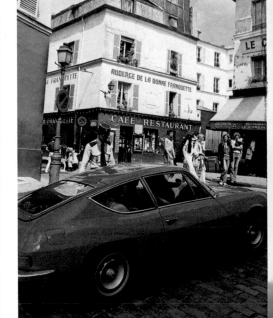

From the early 19th century until the 1920s migration to Montparnasse, Montmartre *on these pages* was the great art colony of Paris and today, despite the fact that the great resident artists (men such as Berlioz, Nerval and Apollinaire) have been driven away by the twin waves of speculation and tourism, the old village has retained its bohemian atmosphere, artists still display their canvasses in the streets and the Place du Tertre is still the epitome of the Paris most people carry in their dreams.

Paris night life, world famous since the 19th century birth of the can-can in the celebrated Moulin Rouge, still reflects the Parisian zest for living in a dazzling array of cafés, nightclubs and bars.

Lighting like that in the Place de la Concorde *overleaf* is very much part of the ancient magic of Paris. The romantic title, 'City of Light' refers not only to the levity and the learning associated with the city but also literally to the fact that in the 18th century Paris was lit by metal oil lamps which provided mirrored illuminations of a kind that had never before been witnessed.

Cafés line the great boulevards, parks and squares. It is here that the Parisians themselves spend much of their time watching and reflecting on the activities of the streets and here too, that much of Parisian intellectual and artistic life has been engendered.

Famous cafés like the Deux Magots *left*, which derived its name from two oriental figures (magots) on the sign of a Chinese silk shop that stood here in the 19th century, have long been meeting places for philosophers, artists and writers.

Paris is a city steeped in beautiful
architecture ranging from the white stone
basilica of the Sacré-Coeur *left and below
right*, a compelling mixture of Byzantine
and Romanesque styles, to Les Invalides
*below*, initiated by Louis XIV in 1671 to
house his wounded soldiers and crowned
by a cupola beneath which lies the tomb of
Napoleon I. Many of these buildings are set
in beautiful, meticulously kept gardens:
viewed from the Eiffel Tower *above* the
Champs de Mars stretch away to the
distant outline of the École Militaire and
beyond the manicured lawns of the
Luxembourg gardens *right* rises the
imposing palace, built in 1615 for Marie de
Medici, wife of Henri IV.
Even the Parisian underground stations
*overleaf* possess their own distinctive
charm. Indeed the most widely visible
reminders of the age of Art Nouveau are
the many surviving Métro entrances like
the one shown *top right*, designed by
Hector Guimard in 1900 for the Paris
Métro Company.

For many the name of Paris conjures up an image of the Seine *above and left.* The ancient buildings, the riverboats, the changes of colour reflected in the water, the gardens and the thirty-two bridges compose one of the world's grandest but most endearing cityscapes.

Yet Paris as a whole is a living work of art. Near the heart of the Latin Quarter Saint-Germain des Près *above right* is the oldest church in Paris. A fine example of Romanesque architecture, during the Revolution it was used as a saltpetre store and today houses the tomb of Descartes.

The Opéra *right,* the neo-baroque masterpiece of Charles Garnier, is a splendid monument to the Second Empire while *below* the beautiful fountain of the four corners of the world stands in the Luxembourg gardens.

Maxim's restaurant in the Rue Royale is a renowned gourmet's paradise *below right.*

Despite the apparent congestion of the Paris skyline *bottom right,* this is a city of open spaces. The Bois de Boulogne *above and left* provides an idyllic spot for relaxation and the Parisians have known how to make the most of their river *top right and below,* which is walled in along its length by expansive stone quays frequently lined with trees.
*Overleaf:* Soldiers of the Republican Guard parade past Notre-Dame.

Pavement cafés provide the opportunity to watch the never-ending pageant of the Paris streets, for its shopping arcades and side streets are a constant hive of activity and its boulevards are the setting for such exciting spectacles as the conclusion of the Tour de France cycle race.

The architecture of Paris' historical and administrative buildings is striking for the magnitude and grandeur of for example, the spacious hall of the Stock Exchange *above* or the Palais-Bourbon which was seized during the Revolution and which now houses the Chamber of Deputies *left* and the Senate *right*.

The imposing gateway *below* marks the entrance to Les Invalides, a collection of enormous buildings, which were all completed in the space of five years.

DAGUESSEAU  LHOPITAL  COLBERT  M<sup>re</sup> MOLÉ  MALESHERBES

The Place de la Concorde *on these pages*, most beautiful by night when the 600 odd lamps and spotlights throughout the square glow like giant fireflies, was once the site of the dreaded guillotine and witness to over 1300 executions. Today its focal point is a 3000 year-old obelisk glorifying Rameses II, which was given to Charles X of France by the Viceroy of Egypt in 1829.

The tower of Notre-Dame provides a magnificent view *overleaf* of Paris with its ancient heart, the Île de la Cité.

In the soft light of floodlit fountains or the last rays of a setting sun or illuminated by a dazzling fireworks display, Gustave Eiffel's 7000 ton masterpiece of engineering assumes a grace and beauty of its own.

The houses of Chanel *above and right* and
Dior *below* with their expensive couture
epitomize the fashion-consciousness of
Paris, the fashion centre of the world.
The same love of elegance finds its
expression in the décor of the sumptuous
onyx-balustraded staircase of the Opéra
*left* and in the evening dress of the
immaculate opera-goers.

Paris has remained a thriving trading city with a multitude of markets, shops and eating places deep in cellars, in the underground and in the most unexpected places. Whatever their location however, the shop windows are a minor art form in themselves.

Longchamps *right* attracts a wide variety of smartly-dressed racing enthusiasts *below* while others take their ease in La Grande Cascade *above*.

In the Place des Pyramides *left* the golden statue of the warrior saint, Joan of Arc, still draws followers of a different kind while the Republican Guard *below left* passes the statue of Charlemagne, the great Frankish emperor.

Dating from the mid 13th century, the huge, delicate vault of La Sainte Chapelle *overleaf* is lit from all sides by the oldest and most sublime stained glass in Paris.

The quarter-mile long palace of Versailles *on these pages and overleaf,* built of pink and cream stone in the style of the classical period of the French Renaissance, is one of the wonders of France. Originally a modest hunting lodge, it was transformed into a vast and splendid palace with sumptuous state apartments by Louis XIV, who moved his household of 20,000 people from the Louvre to the opulent surroundings created by Le Vau, Mansart and Le Brun. No less luxurious are the gardens laid out in the 1660s by Le Nôtre. Studded with statues like that of the Sun King himself *above* or of Diana, the huntress *below,* they also encompass the Grand and the Petit Trianon. In the Queen's House in the Petit Trianon *above left* Marie Antoinette played the role of tenant farmer in the romanticized setting of a poor hamlet *below left,* intended as an escape from the splendour and the etiquette of the main palace.

First published in Great Britain 1979 by Colour Library International Ltd.
© Illustrations: Colour Library International (U.S.A.) Ltd, 163 East 64th Street, New York 10021.
Colour separations by La Cromolito, Milan, Italy.
Display and filmsetting by Focus Photoset, London, England.
Printed and bound by SAGDOS - Brugherio (MI), Italy.
Published by Crescent Books, a division of Crown Publishers Inc.
Library of Congress Catalogue Card No. 79-87534
**CRESCENT 1979**